CANADA
A Landscape Portrait

CANADA
A Landscape Portrait

Edited by J. A. Kraulis
Foreword by Robert Fulford

Hurtig Publishers
Edmonton

My debt to the photographers whose work appears here is obvious. Not so obvious is my debt to photographers not included in this book. With the excellent material I received I could have produced two or three books of this same calibre. I'd like to thank the people who referred me to photographers: Arnet Sheppard, Viki Colledge, Eric Uhman, Roy Edgell, Steve Pigeon, Valerie Wilkinson, Derek Trask, Martin Ingels, Bayne Stanley, and Alan Grogan. As well, many of the photographers whose work is in the book alerted me to others. If I have overlooked anybody I can only apologize by saying that one tends to overlook the most obvious. Thanks also to David Shaw, Sarah Reid, and especially to my wife Linda Küttis.

Hurtig Publishers Ltd.
10560 – 105 Street
Edmonton, Alberta

Canadian Cataloguing in Publication Data

Main entry under title:
Canada, a landscape portrait

ISBN 0-88830-220-7

1. Canada—Description and travel—
1950–   —Views.   2. Photography—Landscapes.
I. Kraulis, J. A., 1949–
FC59.C36   779'.991704644   C82-091196-8
F1016.C36

Foreword

History strives earnestly to teach us its enduring lessons, but in Canada geography is our real teacher, the one to which we must listen with the greatest care. It is geography which sets the tone of Canadian life just as it sets the rules of our working lives and governs our economic relations with other countries. Perhaps the Japanese can mostly ignore their own terrain; possibly Austrians can shove the geography of Austria to the margin of their national consciousness. But Canadians have no such choice. The history of our culture is the history of our attempt to come to terms imaginatively with the variety and vastness of the Canadian landscape — a process which even now may be only in its preliminary stages. In Canada it is of course possible to live a mainly urban life, and in this generation most of us do so. It is also possible to ignore, in one's daily work and recreation, the size of Canada. But inside the unconscious of even the most citified Canadian sits the vast and almost unimaginable empire that we govern. Its presence colours all that we do and feel; it shapes our politics, our public philosophy, our poetry, our very selves. In 1946 Wyndham Lewis, the English novelist and painter, wrote: "Canada will always be so infinitely bigger physically than the small nation that lives in it, even if its population is doubled, that this monstrous, empty habitat must continue to dominate this nation psychologically, and so culturally." A visitor with the sensitive nerve-ends of an artist, Lewis grasped the central point of the country in which he spent the Second World War. But few foreigners ever quite understand the force of Canadian geography. Canadians, for our part, have it in our bones, yet find difficulty articulating our feelings about it.

The most impressive work of Canadian art I have ever seen is an official map of Canada I once encountered in a government boardroom in Ottawa. It was about nine feet high and thirty or so feet across. As I stood before it at mid-point, with my nose almost touching it, my eyes met what most of us would call "the North" — indeed, a place much farther north than most Canadians have ever been. But the real north still went on and on, above my head, towards the ceiling of the room. Southern Ontario, where I have spent most of my life, was a tiny corner at my right foot; the heavily settled part of British Columbia was another tiny corner far to my left. The cities in which most Canadians live, right up to Edmonton, made only a small strip near the floor.

The map had no specific relationship to the purposes of the room in which I found it, and I assume it was put there simply to remind the bureaucrats who used the room of the lengths to which their imaginations must stretch to encompass the reality of Canada. Try as we may, Canadians cannot ignore this reality, but so far we have reached only a dim understanding of how it conditions us.

For generations the study of Canadian history consisted mainly of showing how our country was shaped from the outside — how France and Britain and then the United States manipulated the conditions of our existence. The story of that historic dependency, and of our glacial movement towards independence, is important, but as we told and re-told it we failed to understand the internal reality, the mythic power of the land itself. We came to believe (as many of us believe yet) that if only we could understand the foreigners dominating us, and perhaps understand our own failure to resist them, we would somehow come to a realization of our own identity. We made the common mistake of believing that we could define ourselves exclusively by our relation to others. Only a handful of white Canadians — some explorers, later some entrepreneurs, later still some artists — understood what the natives knew all along, that we were at the mercy of our geography and for good or ill we would be moulded by it. A. R. M. Lower stated the conventional theme of his classic history of Canada in the political terms of his title, *Colony to Nation*; but he concluded by pointing towards a future in which Canadians would come to terms with the Canadian land-mass: "Canada with its division of races presents no common denominator in those profundities which normally unite, in race, language, religion, history and culture. If a common focus is to be found, it must come out of the common homeland itself. If the Canadian people are to find their soul, they must seek for it not in the English language, or the French, but in the little ports of the Atlantic provinces, in the flaming autumn maples of the St. Lawrence Valley, in the portages and lakes of the Canadian Shield, in the sunsets and relentless cold of the prairies, in the foothill, mountain and sea of the west and in the unconquerable vastness of the north. From the land, Canada, must come the soul of Canada."

If that was true when Lower wrote it in 1946, it is far more true today. Canada has developed in the last three decades perhaps the most liberal immigration policies in the world. Unlike other democracies of the West, Canada does not temporarily import "guest workers," use their talents, and then send them home when they are not wanted. Instead it offers the gift of full citizenship — and many, from all over the world, eagerly accept that gift. The result is that the growing population lacks a shared pre-Canadian background; all that Canadians have in common (and it is, I argue, a great deal) is the physical fact of Canada and the opportunities that fact offers.

Since Lower wrote, Canadians have spent some considerable time in search of the soul he imagined; what we have found has so far surprised us, and in some cases alarmed us. Slowly we are beginning to understand what a Canadian is, but that turns out to be different from what we expected. We are a "nation," but not in the sense that history (mostly European history) taught us to use that word. Conditioned by our experience of and our reading about nineteenth-century nations, we expected that a mature Canada would resemble those earlier nations in certain essential ways. Canadians would, for instance, develop a patriotism more or less binding on all citizens; we would develop a point of view, perhaps an ideology. We would have an identity. But maturity for Canada has turned out to be something new under the sun, something for which the history of others could not prepare us.

Public policy, in everything from railway construction to broadcasting regulation, has urged us in the direction of unity; instead we have grown more diverse. Public policy has tried to elicit agreement on methods of national development; instead we have tended to disagree more and more, and to make our disagreements more vocal. Public policy in Ottawa has pushed for centralization of power; instead the regions of Canada have become more self-consciously separate. Our most characteristic public forum is the First Ministers Conference, at which provincial premiers become television stars, each with a performance to give, each with a set of regional or provincial grievances to state, each with an audience back home to please. And the focus of our national public life is not the improvement of our general condition but rather the appropriate method of dividing the revenues from our natural resources. The issues dictated by geography overcome all other issues, moving back and forth across party lines, so that socialists and conservatives from one region, while disagreeing on all else, find themselves in agreement on their region's entitlement to the fruits of the earth. All the calculations of political scientists and historians are defeated by the brute facts of the Canadian terrain. Michael Bliss, the historian, recognized this when he described the federal Geological Survey as "that little band of explorers who have done as much to map our national identity as all our writers and artists combined." The identity the geologists map is the same identity we see displayed at the First Ministers Conference.

What is at work here is not the frustration of a benign national purpose by fractious regionalists; it is the inevitable development of a pluralistic society coming to terms with the proprietorship of an empire. The force of our geography has not been diminished by modern communications, as many once thought it would be. Mass communications have instead made us all more conscious of our rights and our separate identities; they have reinforced rather than dissolved our demands by providing us with the means to express our feelings. At the same time, they have helped us to find pleasure in our diversity. In an earlier time many a theorist of mass media guessed that television would smooth out regional differences and create a bland sameness across society. But something like the opposite has happened. While television has taught us to know each other better, it has heightened our awareness of one another. And jet aircraft, while they take us swiftly from place to place, don't make us want to eliminate the distinctions between regions. A Torontonian and a Newfoundlander can now visit each other with some ease, but each in the end will probably decide that what makes the other valuable is his separate and different existence. It is only in the age of mass communications that genuine pluralism can flourish, because it is only in this age that we have the means to learn about each other.

The size of our country and its physical variety, combined with democratic traditions, have created a unique political and social atmosphere. A dozen years ago, when I was counselling American draft dodgers on their future in this country, I caught a glimpse of Canada as it must seem to outsiders who have personal reasons to be concerned about the openness of Canadian life. The draft dodgers were escaping from forced military service, of course, but I discovered among them a good many who had other concerns; there were even some who were physically ineligible for the army but who had declared themselves "draft dodgers" anyway and had crossed the border. What they were fleeing, no matter their politics (and some were far more conservative than I had expected), was the pressure of American political opinion. In the United States they had felt called upon to commit themselves to political factions, whether they wanted to or not, because American public life demanded commitment to this or that point of view. What they noticed first about Canada was the absence of a compulsion to conform. They discovered to their surprise that patriotism is not a prerequisite of Canadian citizenship. What the draft dodgers found in Canada was a unique kind of psychic freedom, a rather different matter from political freedom. It is this freedom, expressed in ethnic, linguistic, and regional terms, that forms the real basis of Canadian life.

The curious fact is that in order to qualify as Canadians we are not required to be loyal, even in theory, to the idea of Canada. At an editorial meeting at *Maclean's* early in the 1960s, the then-new subject of Quebec separatism was introduced. One editor declared firmly that separatists should be prosecuted for treason. He was an English immigrant, still innocent in Canadian ways, and his suggestion was greeted with derisive laughter, but it occurred to me at the time that if one looked at his views from a global perspective they were not altogether preposterous. In a very few countries would the idea of national dismemberment be greeted with such insouciance. But in fact, by unspoken agreement, Canadian citizenship carries the ultimate freedom: the freedom to declare that one doesn't want to be a Canadian, to urge that one's region should cease to be part of Canada, and yet to go on being a Canadian and receiving the appropriate benefits. No Quebec or Alberta separatist, so far as I know, has been denied a federal welfare payment or even a Canada Council grant because of his or her desire to separate.

This is the openness which the draft dodgers found at first rather baffling and then engaging. It is an openness which some Canadians find vexing, and which makes our public life unpredictable. It even makes it possible for the leader of the allegedly federalist party in Quebec, the provincial Liberals, to explain constantly that his loyalty to Canada is contingent and may be withdrawn at any moment. This relaxed and almost casual style of public discourse has always created difficulties and always will. Nevertheless, we should cherish it: nothing is closer to the essence of Canada, and nothing makes a greater contribution to the freedom of the Canadian citizen.

Out of the immense problems created by our geography, we have made a political system based on severely limiting the power of each level of government. It is commonly assumed in Canada that the individual is more important than the state, no matter how powerful the state becomes, and that one's private life is more important than one's public life. These assumptions flow directly from the troublesome but finally beneficial contest between the centralizing force of Ottawa and the disparate forces which stubbornly resist the central government. We understand, without having to articulate it, that it is as Canadian to resist Ottawa as to support it. This struggle is so all-encompassing that it touches every aspect of our lives: it affects the individual because it cripples the psychological power of government. When a country's government is so clearly split, so obviously at war with itself, it is unable to impose conformity on the citizens. In these terms, federal-provincial conflict can be seen as one of the keys to individual liberty. To a foreigner it may seem odd — even perverse — that Canadians so often vote for one party provincially and another party federally, but this is no more than the Canadian way of keeping government in its place.

The vastness of Canada has made this federal-provincial balance both possible and necessary: Canada as a unitary state would be a nightmare of bureaucracy. But while our size effectively brakes most of the excesses of government, it has an even more striking effect on political ideas. When they arrive in Canada, political ideas change. The harsh demand and the urgent appeal are dissipated by the size of the country; radicalism of left or right turns up in one region or another from time to time, but no truly radical idea has ever seized the country as a whole. Neither of the two great malevolent myths of the twentieth century, communism and fascism, has developed a sizeable following in Canada. Political movements which set out to swallow the country are instead swallowed up themselves, lost somewhere over the prairies. A neat, compact European country can generate among its citizens enough agreement to bring even the most terrifyingly brutal idea to power, but in Canada too many countervailing forces are at work. In this, as in so many other ways, Canadians are more fortunate than most of their fellow citizens of the globe.

This is true even of specific and apparently manageable issues, and even among people one might expect to agree easily. In Vancouver today liberal, enlightened opinion believes that the Newfoundland harp seal hunt is barbarous and should be outlawed; in St. John's, liberal, enlightened opinion believes precisely the opposite. What the people of one area regard as wise, the people of another may see as ridiculous.

Once, when I tried to explain Canadian cultural nationalism of the 1970s to an art college seminar in Halifax, I found that the whole nationalist movement — developed by dozens of artists across the country over several years — was dismissed as "Ontario politics." A political generality which seems strikingly true in Prince George may appear shaky when it reaches Thunder Bay, rather dubious when it gets to Chicoutimi, and outlandish when it is heard in Cornerbrook.

This means that in Canada no proposition can be finally binding, no argument settled, no plan totally agreed upon. For that reason Canada offers an especially frustrating life to intellectuals, whose training is usually based on European or American models. At some point in their careers, having absorbed foreign experience, they turn to their own country and attempt to impose on it patterns and ideologies developed elsewhere.

They almost always break their swords. They discover that Canadians can't or won't make hard decisions; that every idea approved in one part of Canada is cancelled out by another part. Canada, because of its size and diversity, is not a country of *either/or* but a country of *maybe* and *I hope perhaps*. This is a basic fact of our nature, but to intellectuals it appears as nothing more than a form of spinelessness. Intellectuals want clear definitions, and Canada can't provide them. Leslie Armour, professor of philosophy at the University of Ottawa, is just such an intellectual. Armed with his Ph.D. from the University of London, he brings the full weight of the western philosophical tradition to bear on the problems currently besetting Canadian life. In his *The Idea of Canada and the*

Crisis of Community (1981), he examines our life as a nation and (no surprise!) finds us wanting. Canada is disintegrating, he says, because we haven't evolved a common view of ourselves and our future. He notes that we come together — sometimes — when faced with a threat from outside, but "this is not enough to make a nation. To have a nation there must be a tendency toward a common strategy." Intellectuals adopt this theme when commenting on every area of our national life, from secondary manufacturing to mass culture. An economist seeking to revive our sickly manufacturing sector will talk endlessly of "industrial strategy" (which means emphasizing one industry at the expense of another, and usually one region at the expense of another). A cultural bureaucrat trying to make sense of, say, Canadian television will write papers about long-range planning and the political will required to support it. Canadians will hear these views, nod in apparent agreement, then ignore what has been said — and the politicians, sensing the national attitude, will do the same. In place of the central planning and ruthless decision-making favoured by the Japanese and the West Germans, Canadians put their faith in luck and improvisation. A common strategy — even a tendency towards a common strategy — is precisely what Canadians, collectively, do not want and never have wanted, except perhaps in wartime. This has been the case for so long that it must be a part of our national character, and to ignore it when considering the fate of Canada is to miss the essence.

On the last page of his rather melancholy book, Leslie Armour declares: "We must, indeed, eventually decide what we want."

Au contraire, it is just by declining to make that sort of decision that we have so far survived. Even those institutions which have endured in Canada for centuries — the Crown, for example — have rarely been subjected to careful examination or defined with care. No one can say what the Crown means to Canadians in 1982, anymore than anyone could say what it meant in 1922; we avoid deciding upon that definition precisely because to do so would be divisive. Were we to make a national decision (abolish the monarchy, say, or, on the other hand, place it squarely at the symbolic core of the country), we would require assent from all the regions of Canada, and not all the regions would be able to give assent. Ergo, the Crown is allowed to float free above Canada, neither quite rejected nor quite embraced; every Canadian is thus permitted his own view of the Crown, as of so many other things.

One of the few intellectuals who understood this, almost from the beginning of his career, was Mackenzie King. He drove the most thoughtful of his fellow citizens almost mad with rage by adamantly refusing to make the decisions that they thought needed to be made. When King died, the socialist poet F. R. Scott wrote a bitter memorial tribute:

He blunted us.

We had no shape
Because he never took sides,
And no sides
Because he never allowed them to take shape.

A cruel indictment, and not altogether inaccurate, yet King governed Canada during some of its most painful years, and left it intact. It was King's party, not Scott's CCF, that successfully (if rather surreptitiously) brought the welfare state to Canada. And King's most persistent and brilliant critic during his career, the historian Frank H. Underhill, acknowledged at the end of the day that it was King, not Underhill, who understood how to govern Canada.

That aspect of life that intellectuals most enjoy and admire — the sharp clash of ideas, the articulation of fully developed ideologies — was precisely what King laboured to avoid. No wonder we hated him, and hate his memory still. Someday a thorough search of King's diaries — that vast ocean of insight, gossip, and malice, cumulatively the most important work of literature in our history — may finally reveal his secret. How did he see so deeply into the nature of his country? Perhaps he himself never consciously grasped the quality of his own genius. Perhaps King's ascension to power and his ability to hold it were produced by the fortuitous conjunction — so rare in history — of an unshaped, inarticulate people and a leader who perfectly embodied his nation's character.

Plutarch says of the geographers of the ancient world that they would "crowd into the edges of their maps parts of the world which they do not know about, adding notes in the margin to the effect that beyond this lies nothing but sandy deserts full of wild beasts, and unapproachable bogs." In the mind of the modern Canadian, the map of his own country has many such edges, each of them filled with images (accumulated since childhood) of vast empty wastelands beyond the horizon, uninhabited and therefore uninhabitable. The maps prepared by our cartographers are accurate and detailed, but our spiritual maps have much in common with those of Plutarch's time. Now and then word comes back to us — from an artist or an explorer — that some empty space on our map is in fact filled with life, and mentally we adjust our conception of that one place. But the process is necessarily slow. A Canadian comes into the world with a spatial imagination no larger than that of a Belgian or a Greek, but to understand his own country he must stretch that imagination to its limits. He may find it easier simply to ignore or belittle most of the country, and in this the Europeans long ago set an example for us: it was Voltaire in *Candide* (1759) who had a shrewd, cynical character describe Canada as "a few acres of snow." But those of us who have inherited those acres of snow, or who have adopted them by moving here from somewhere else, cannot so casually dismiss our surroundings. If we wish truly to inhabit Canada, rather than simply to live in some circumscribed area of it, then we need to fill those empty acres imaginatively. We can do this only through art, and art of a particular kind. Landscape painting and photography, nature poetry, novels like W. O. Mitchell's that set down on paper the style of a terrain — these are the means by which human beings take spiritual possession of territory. Before we can finally take Canada into our minds we need to experience it through art; in effect, artists must invent it for us.

This was the central insight of the Group of Seven, who made it their business to display the landscape of Canada to the people who controlled it. In this the Group was not entirely original: there had been landscape painters in Canada for centuries, and one artist after another had tried to set down with oil paint or watercolour the essence of the country. In most cases they had brought to Canada the manners of European art; the Canadian landscape as they recorded it had a gentle, romantic air. While the members of the Group of Seven also drew a great deal from the European tradition, they set for themselves a sterner artistic task. They shaped their style to fit the material, producing a rugged and even (by the standards of their time) a brutal art. Working together, exchanging ideas constantly, they moved forward like mountain climbers linked by rope, developing what would become almost a religion. In their view, the Canadian landscape deserved no less. Tom Thomson (who died in 1917, three years before the Group was officially formed), Lawren Harris, A. Y. Jackson, and the others eventually produced a challenging visual account of the physical fact of Canada. In their hands, central and northern Ontario, the Rockies, and the Arctic became the setting for a great and vigorous artistic drama.

Their paintings shocked some of the first to see them, but before many years had passed the Group received an astonishing reward for their labours. Though they never achieved more than fleeting recognition outside Canada, within it they became the most remarkable success in the history of our culture. No other artists — in music or literature or any other medium — have had such an impact. No others have appealed simultaneously to rich patrons, schoolchildren, their fellow artists, and the public in general. No others have maintained their status over six decades. The Group of Seven captured the imagination of Canada in a way that it has never otherwise been captured, before or since.

This success was not an accident produced by publicity or the machinations of art dealers; had it been, it would have slipped away when the early Group of Seven paintings grew old and the painters, one by one, died. But the popularity of the Group has instead grown with every passing decade; by the time Harris and Jackson died in the 1970s, they were treated as national heroes, their obituaries running as long as those of generals or statesmen. The Group had become part of the cultural myth of a whole people.

When Canadians looked at the Group of Seven's paintings they experienced a rare moment of self-recognition, and they continued to have this experience whenever they returned to the art. They saw in those hundreds of paintings and sketches a vision of the Canadian spirit as formed by the Canadian landscape. As a result, the Group has inspired generations of artists — not only painters but also film-makers, photographers (including some whose work is in this book), and illustrators. It is even arguable that their influence has moved into literature; certainly Canadian literature continues to exhibit an exceptionally close relationship with Canadian geography. "Everything that is central in Canadian writing," Northrop Frye tells us, "seems to be marked by the imminence of the natural world." Even though Canada in the twentieth century became more and more a country of city-dwellers, art and literature continued to find their focus in natural settings. This was not nostalgia for the audience's or the artists' rural backgrounds; it was part of a continuing attempt to come to terms with the country.

From the beginning, Canadian artists have at the same time reacted against the use of the landscape in Canadian art. "Every damned tree in the country has now been painted," a young rebel on the Toronto art scene commented in the 1950s, and in doing so spoke for a whole generation that at first had found the Group of Seven oppressive. For these artists the Group's tradition, far from opening up new frontiers to art, seemed on the contrary to foreclose possibilities by dictating a narrow view of artistic possibilities in Canada. In the 1950s and 1960s, abstractionism was fuelled by international sources of inspiration and reflected mainly the newer urban reality — or seemed to do so for a time. But even the most urbanized of artists ended up by returning in his or her own fashion to the landscape and its continuing impact on Canadians. The generation that started out by reacting against the Group ended up by embracing it. In Toronto an artist like Gordon Rayner, after drawing on all the techniques of abstraction developed in New York, and using them brilliantly, returned — just like the Group of Seven — to the central Ontario bush for the background to his most impressive canvases. Michael Snow is above all other things an urban intellectual, but when he took a major exhibition to Paris he included in it a re-interpretation of the Group of Seven's insights. Harold Town, who in his early career saw little value in the Group's heritage, eventually wrote a compelling and important book on Tom Thomson. Joyce Wieland, whose first canvases were as far from the Group as it was possible for them to be, later turned to film-making and used the myth of Tom Thomson — as well as his physical surroundings — as the basis for her feature film, *The Far Shore*.

Meanwhile, the painters who consistently appealed to a large public — for instance, Toni Onley in Vancouver and the late William Kurelek in Toronto — were those who found fresh ways to interpret the Canadian landscape; Onley through the lovely haze of a gentle, English-influenced manner, Kurelek in the rough but expressive terms of the self-taught primitive.

Each of these artists encountered the land in personal terms. Kurelek, who grew up in deprived circumstances on a prairie farm in the Depression, was telling the public his own story as much as the land's; in the process he became perhaps the most universally admired artist of his generation as well as the most successful book illustrator in Canada. Kurelek reflected in his work a quality that eastern city-dwellers have often noted in westerners: they are closer to the land, not so much in space as in time. Even that majority which has no direct experience of rural life carries a folk memory of breaking the plains: an accountant in Calgary, say, is the grandson of a pioneer, and his childhood memories include stories of the heroic age of western development. Even in the 1980s, the remembered vision of the prairie as virginal and untouched — menacing in its way, and yet conveying enormous promise — is always just on the edge of the conversation.

For an artist like Joyce Wieland, who grew up in Toronto, the experience is different but no less profound. In her case the encounter with the landscape is a matter of consciously seeking out the background to Canadian life. Her work may in some ways reflect a more romantic view of the landscape, but it remains a view that places the natural world at the core of Canadian consciousness.

The function of art is to make life comprehensible and bearable, but the function of these particular artists is to resolve the tension within us between the enormity of Canada and our urgent need to encompass it. The size of Canada, and the emptiness of it, George Woodcock has noted, are two facts that are often present in the mind of every Canadian. To make art out of that emptiness, to humanize nature — to deny, in fact, that the country is empty — is a supremely human act, an act which is required of the Canadian imagination if the country is to realize its own artistic possibilities.

In the end the need to know Canada's physical nature is crucial to our future because it is in the land that we can find the grounds for genuine optimism. Native mythology, to which few of us pay sufficient attention, has always insisted that life will be governed by the natural world; it has always drawn its symbols from the immediate landscape, and carried the powerful implication that an understanding of human conduct can be drawn from that landscape. And from the moment when the earliest explorers were swallowed up by the apparently endless St. Lawrence River, the land has been the basis for hope. In later generations it was always the astonishing gift of our geography that stimulated the ambitions of Canadian — in one era the abundance of fish in the waters, in another the opening of the west to agriculture, in another John Diefenbaker's northern vision, in still another the slow unfolding of the Arctic's infinite promises of resource development.

The incredible space on earth which history absent-mindedly gave us has laid down the rules of Canada's existence: it determines the content of parliamentary debates as much as it determines the content of our art galleries; it has protected our freedom and made us, in comparison with almost any other peoples in the world, enviably wealthy. It is our heritage and our problem and the source of our future happiness. Perhaps we shall never come to terms with it intimately; but it is the task and privilege of the present generation, in the midst of our self-generated tensions and conflicts, to move still closer to an understanding of what this geographic empire means to us and to our descendants. James Reaney, that remarkable poet who has written so often and so well on Canada, has given us a brief account of a childhood memory; it might be called The Birth of a Canadian Imagination. "I can remember as a child looking at a map of Canada at school and wolfing down the whole thing as *my* country. The shape of Hudson Bay, the Northern Arctic islands, the coast of Labrador and the shapes of the Great Lakes were particularly lovable. Quebec always seemed like the profile of — someone — the Duchess in *Alice in Wonderland* with the Ottawa River defining her chin and jaws, Cape Jones as her nose, Labrador as her head-dress and some unknown river (the Nottaway) as the outline of her rather pursed mouth. Ontario seems like someone in a rather grotesque rocking chair. The Arctic Islands had the fascinating fretted shapes of mackerel clouds in a sunset. Naturally I have never since known Canada as well as I did then."

Robert Fulford

11

Introduction

In Canada, it is still possible for a person to climb to the summit of a mountain, a singularly conspicuous and prominent place, and stand where no one has ever stood before. On a clear day, the view in every direction might stretch a hundred miles and more. It would be a view seen for the first time: a view no one had ever laid eyes on before.

To see that which has never been seen before is an exhilarating experience; an almost religious one for some, a heightened feeling of having a privileged part in the expanding consciousness of an unfathomably rich and extraordinary universe. It is an experience that demands a place in memory, and more, it is an experience that demands to be shared.

To see, to show what has in some sense not been seen before is the mission of photography. Those who photograph the landscape do not, of course, need to stand where no one else has stood, confronting a view no one else has seen. This is neither a necessary nor a sufficient condition for the creation of photographs of value and power, photographs which are more than mere records. But landscape photography shares one quality with the first ascent of a remote mountain: both are experiences imbued with the spirit of discovery, the quest to know the land.

An art is influenced and inspired by its context, the backdrop against which it is created. For landscape photography in Canada, this backdrop is a country where great mountains remain unclimbed: a country where the primal elements from which landscapes evolve — stone, ice, and water — have interacted on a vaster scale than anywhere else; a country where the dramatic meeting of earth and ocean takes place along a coastline twice as long as that of any other nation; a country with more fresh water in its lakes than exists in all other countries combined. Canada is a land with room for extreme opposites: the dense, forbidding rain forests of the west coast and the stark, wide-open barren-lands of the Arctic; the absolutely flat horizon of parts of the prairies and some of the world's highest plumb-vertical cliffs on Baffin Island; the brilliant autumn foliage of eastern deciduous forests and the unrelieved pristine white of immense icefields in the Yukon and the Northwest Territories; the relentless thunder of great waterfalls and the total, perfect silence of winter in the wilderness when the wind stops. It is a land, particularly when population and politics are taken into account, with more freedom of space than any other.

Few photographers have travelled the full extent of Canada. None have seen all of its major features, and none ever will; the country is simply too big. In fact, it would be difficult even to find anyone who has visited the four compass-point extremes, the easternmost, westernmost, southernmost, and northernmost places in Canada. For those who photograph any part of this land, the land itself constitutes a formidable heritage.

The confidence and maturity of an art derives in part from its heritage, its immediate and permanent source. One should expect, then, that the body of Canadian landscape photography is extraordinarily rich in both quality and quantity.

This is not to imply that a small country cannot foster great landscape photography. Indeed, both because good photography looks ever deeper into ever more familiar worlds, and because no photographer could hope to explore all of Canada, the size and diversity of the country is, on a certain ordinary level, irrelevant. But on a more intangible, deeper level, it is unavoidably significant. A photographer cannot help but be proud in the knowledge that he must live up to high standards, that the subject matter he has to work with is as sublime as any there is. Even if one never has the privilege of standing on top of a previously unclimbed mountain, it is reassuring — and inspiring — to know that it is there.

This is a collection of individual discoveries in the Canadian landscape, highlights in the ever-changing, infinitely manifold drama of the land preserved and expressed with skill and sensitivity; prominent memorials from between infinite horizons.

The land, our immediately accessible universe, is, like the universe, mystical, mysterious, and ultimately unknowable. It is implied by forces and structures which constitute landscape, the subject matter portrayed in this book. Landscape is generally thought of as being synonymous with scenery, but, for the photographer, it is a great deal more profound than that. The question of scale, for example, is irrelevant when one seeks to show essence, rather than mere appearance. A careful study of frost-split stone can be more revealing of process, more evocative of place than a casual snapshot of miles of tundra. What counts in a strong image is not the grandeur of identifiable landmarks, but rather how convincingly and clearly the image confronts us with a manifestation of the land, how well it communicates the universal instead of the specific.

The word "art," in a narrow sense, denotes specifically fine art, the kind meant to be hung on a wall or to be displayed on a pedestal or in a glass case. This can be done with photography; it is obviously one of the visual arts. But its membership in that family is an awkward one; too often it is compared and even equated with painting. Like the constant comparison of a younger sibling to an older, this is often insensitive, inappropriate, and simply irrelevant.

It is not totally invalid, however, to compare photography with painting. Beaudelaire wrote of the correspondence that unites all the arts and life; of how their division into separate categories is in a sense artificial and obscures their unity on deeper, more profound levels. Moreover, the visual arts are often intermixed to the extent that clear demarcations between different media do not exist: photographs have been painted over, oils and silk screens have been derived from photographs. From the standpoint of the viewer, as distinguished from that of the creator, it makes some sense to evaluate photographs as one would paintings: both are essentially two-dimensional rectangular images which can be analysed using a certain visual vocabulary — line, colour, form, composition, perspective, and so on — and interpreted with reference to reality and imagination.

However, in certain fundamental aspects photography admits no parallels with painting and is perhaps far more appropriately compared with other arts. Unlike painting, photography involves no practiced hand skills. Like writing, it is basically a mental discipline, assisted not infrequently by research.

While a painting can show action caught at an optimum instant, timing is not an underlying factor in the painter's work; in principle, a painting could be created on any occasion, spread over any period. The creation of a photograph, on the other hand, shares with the performance of music an understood basic concern with the magic of a moment; a concern that has as much importance in landscape photography as in any other kind of photography, except some types of commercial work.

Photography is particularly close in spirit to music in several other respects. Both the musician who plays Beethoven and the photographer who works with an inspiring landscape are not so much developing their own originality as they are interpreting a beautiful thing in such a manner as to do it the most possible justice. Both are striving for an ideal more universal than personal. The musician and the photographer both use highly crafted and precisely adjusted instruments which are essential to the refined standard of their work. With his or her instrument, each explores the infinitesimally delicate nuances of the one basic thing which is the essence of that medium and around which all else — infinite possibilites — are structured. For the musician, the quality of sound is everything. For the photographer, the quality of light is everything. Photography and music are both infused with wonder for the infinite ways in which a single apparently simple energy — sound in one case and light in the other — reveal a profoundly complex universe.

In the final analysis, of course, photography is a medium all its own, with only partial links with any other single medium. Its validity, its value as an art lies precisely in the degree to which it can be differentiated from the other arts. The differences are especially marked in the case of landscape photography. Landscape photographs are at the opposite end of the spectrum from the type of photograph in which the photographer intervenes in the subject matter by manoeuvring it or altering its appearance before it is photographed. This process has been called "making" a photograph as opposed to "taking" one, the idea being that the photographer has *created* what appears in the image as opposed to *discovering* it. The distinction was made elegantly several decades ago by the late American photographer, Phillipe Halsman, who wrote a book around a series of ingenious photographs that were "made." Such photographs, having come into existence through synthesis, most closely relate to the act of painting, even though the usual end result — advertising photography — seems most unlike painting.

The distinction between "making" and "taking" a photograph has come to be emphasized in a totally different way. Any good photograph is "made," rather than simply "taken," the argument goes, the difference being the degree of discipline and care invested by the photographer. While it forms the basis of an excellent teaching slogan, this distinction obscures the earlier, perhaps more useful and valid one, which in its properly critical sense implies no value judgement.

Thus landscape photographs belong to the type of photography which is "taken," or "found," or "given," depending on the metaphor one prefers; the last having been appreciatively used by a number of photographers to acknowledge their debt, their obligation to their subject. Semantics aside, what is significant about landscape photography is that the subject, the essential material, already exists without the intervention of the photographer and is essentially beyond the photographer's ability to change — but not beyond his ability to interpret. How the photographer interprets, how he abstracts an image from the general context, how he discovers and reveals: this informs the character and purpose of his art. The power, the value of landscape photography derives from its direct link with that which really existed.

When we look at a painting, we face the artist; we see his virtuosity, his imagination, his personal statement. When we look at a photograph, we stand beside the photographer and we see the world through his or her eyes. A great photograph is a window opening onto a view of reality that has never been seen quite that way before.

Underlying the effect every landscape photograph achieves is the awareness that what has been photographed was real, that it existed in a time and a place. The effect bounces off that awareness in myriad different ways. Some photos, such as Lance W. Camp's on page 92, or Peter Frank's on page 53, simply evince an immediate "Wow!" by capturing dramatic, elusive phenomena. Some photos bewilder, even frustrate, by refusing to give up answers. George Calef's on page 63 is clearly a photograph and it is a clear photograph, graphic and effective, but what exactly is it? It contains no scale references to tell us whether the photographer was standing on the ground photographing pebbles or whether he was in a helicopter photographing boulders. The picture is complete, yet an enigma. Some photographs surprise by showing something from a new angle, as do Hans Blohm's on page 20 and Catherine M. Young's on page 75; or by juxtaposing two or more contrasting or complementary subjects, as do Calef's (page 48) and John de Visser's (page 45).

What impresses in each case is the idea that reality, when photographed, can look the way it does; that a niche in rock can be so beautiful (Anders Lenes's photograph on page 86); that the Yukon wilderness can appear so clean and simple (Ulrich Kretschmar's photograph on page 78); that erosion can cut so elegant a design (Egon Bork's photograph on page 74).

Gera Dillon's work on page 21 looks like an impressionist painting. It is a straightforward mechanically precise photograph, its "soft" effect created by the real movement in the water and not by unfocusing. Its merit has nothing to do with the idea that a *photograph* can be made to look like a painting; this is easily done by means of various gimmicks which adulterate the true worth and potential of photography. Rather, the photograph impresses because it shows that something *real* in the landscape can look like a painting, which is another matter entirely.

Great photography, needless to say, involves more than simply recording a real scene which is interesting or attractive. There is an immense difference between what the average viewer sees when looking at a photograph and what that viewer would have seen had he or she been where the photo was taken when it was taken. This difference is the measure of the photographer's skill and sensitivity as an artist. It is a difference that depends, in part, on the photographer's trained eye, which, like the musician's trained ear, becomes refined through years of practice.

The trained eyed of the photographer has primarily to do with understanding one's instruments, their characteristics, capabilities, and limitations. The camera and film see the world in a significantly different way than do the eye and mind. It is perhaps a common misconception that the photographer uses the camera to distort or enhance what he photographs. In fact, however, the camera and film see much more accurately and consistently than do the eye and mind. Obtrusive details are recorded unfailingly and proportions and distances are shown exactly as they are, unadjusted in relative importance. Film is sensitive to the colour of light and the contrasts it creates, while the eye adjusts and adapts, generally unaware of significant differences. For example, a photograph taken by the light of one's living-room fixtures with film designed for use in daylight will be grotesquely yellow because the light from ordinary lightbulbs *is* much more yellow than daylight, a fact one's eyes do not normally notice. It is often thought that the photographer compresses, or exaggerates perspective through the use of different lenses. But in fact, by the laws of physics, camera lenses always show true perspective. The photographer controls the perspective on a scene solely by choosing the position of the camera in relation to it. Lenses of different focal lengths will merely determine how much or how little of a scene gets included within the picture frame.

Thus the instruments of photography render the real world with mechanical exactitude and pure objectivity. The nature of the instruments defines the stern challenge and the unique opportunity of the medium. Again as is the case for the musician, the photographer is bound by certain fixed physical properties and laws, constraints which require years of disciplined practice to master.

More than one critic has made the worst

of possible comparisons between photography and painting, namely that like a painting, a photograph can take a great deal of time and deliberate effort to create. Presumably this idea is intended as some sort of reassurance of photography's legitimacy among the fine arts. But it has no meaning, not so much because it is false, but because it is irrelevant. It *can* take a lot of time and effort to create a single photograph, but the length of time or indeed the toil involved would bear no relation to the particular merits of that photo. Among the greatest and most famous of photographs are many that brought the photographer together with his subject for little more than a minute, sometimes less.

Implying that there is any value to the idea that it can take a long time to create a photograph, moreover, denies one of the most important, magical characteristics of photography: its ability to capture the transient moment. The reason many a great photograph has been made quickly is precisely because the window of opportunity in the circumstances of its taking was open so briefly. Some of the shots in this book were available to the photographer for but a few minutes of working time, if that, before disappearing. In the case of the aerial landscapes, the time available for the photographer to make all decisions and to take the photograph was no longer than a few seconds.

Many of the best landscape photographs, like other kinds of photographs, convey a feeling of nostalgia, of sadness for a moment captured but at the same time irrevocably gone.

The idea that a landscape photograph could theoretically have been taken by someone else does not in the least bit diminish the achievement or the credit due to the photographer who took it. Not long ago an articulate and respected critic of photography wrote an opinion about a series of American space photographs which were exhibited in a gallery. The question raised in the essay was whether these photographs had any place in a gallery of photographic art. The point was made that the photographs were not the works of serious photographers; not, therefore, the result of the feeling and vision of sensitive artists.

What was curious about the opinion was not so much its basically untenable implication that art and science are entirely unrelated human endeavours to be separated by an insurmountable non-porous barrier, but rather the idea that the basic value, the inherent meaning of a photograph somehow depends on the credentials of the photographer.

Among the American space photos is the famous one of the sphere of Earth suspended in the black void of space. It is perhaps the ultimate landscape photograph: the ultimate view of the environment taken from the ultimate scenic turnoff. One could argue that, on an emotional as well as on a rational level, this image has changed the consciousness of more people more profoundly than has any other single image produced by man, be it photograph or painting. The idea that it does not belong in the hallowed category of the "art" of photography calls into question not the value of the image so much as it does the value of that particular categorization of "art."

What cannot be overlooked in the case of this photograph is the fact that, no matter who had taken it, the final image would have been essentially the same. The reality the image discovers is so overwhelming, so pure, so compelling that it demands the most direct, simple and obvious treatment. A famous photographer, weeping at the sight, out there on board the space capsule, could not have made a better or a different photograph. The photograph of the Earth from space is not a statement of personal expression, but it does evoke a universal expression of wonder; it is not notable as the creation of one person's mind, but it is a superb celebration of human consciousness. A photograph could not be asked to achieve more.

Many photographers would argue that the art in a photograph, its truth and its beauty, comes not from them but rather through them. It is a notion that identifies photography as a bridge between the two noble functions of human consciousness, the creative and the appreciative. Artists aspire to create. Without anyone to appreciate what they have brought into existence, their work has no meaning. What unites the creator with the appreciator is the sharing of the experience and the spirit of discovery. Landscape photography is the pure art of discovery.

J. A. Kraulis

Gera Dillon/ Evening light on Laurentian hillside, Morin Heights, Quebec

Paul S. Guyot/ Daybreak on Nym Lake, north of Quetico Provincial Park, Ontario

John de Visser/ Overlapping ice floes, new ice, coast of Labrador

Hans Blohm/ Rainbow in the Richardson Mountains, Yukon

Gera Dillon/ Lilypads near Montfort, the Laurentians, Quebec

Jeremy Addington/ Hemlock, Kokanee Creek near Nelson, British Columbia

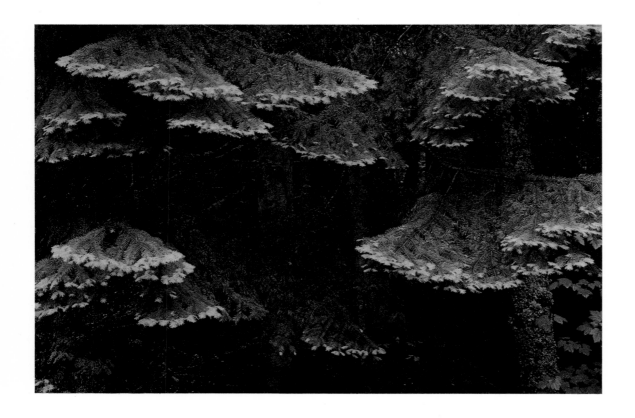

Charlie Clayton/ Forest in early autumn, Thunder Bay, Ontario

Egon Bork/ cattle on rangeland near Manyberries, Alberta

Paul von Baich/ Autumn reflection south of Canoe Lake, Algonquin Provincial Park, Ontario

Richard Vroom/ Farmstead, Borden, Prince Edward Island

Lance W. Camp/Trans-Canada Highway and the Rockies at sundown, west of Calgary, Alberta

John de Visser/ Winter scene in rural New Brunswick

Gera Dillon/ Autumn snowfall at Deer Lake, the Laurentians, Quebec

Menno Fieguth/ Farm west of Drumheller, Alberta

Egon Bork/ Milk River valley, Writing-on-Stone Provincial Park, Alberta

Pat Morrow/ Ski tracks raised
by sun and wind erosion, Forbidden
Plateau, Vancouver Island,
British Columbia

Gunter Marx/ Tulip beds, Fraser valley, British Columbia

Michel Bourque/ Bridge across St. Lawrence River, Trois Rivières, Quebec

Vince Claerhout/ Chinook arch over the Rockies, Pincher Creek, Alberta

Freeman Patterson/Autumn mist, Kingston Creek, Kingston, New Brunswick

Chic Harris/ Country road from Long Reach to Kingston, New Brunswick

Egon Bork/ Frosted field west of Sherwood Park, Alberta

Bob Herger/ Mist and the Fraser River, British Columbia

John de Visser/ The Rockies
near Jasper, Jasper National
Park, Alberta

Lorne Coulson/ Sand dune and black-eyed-Susan, Carberry Sandhills, Manitoba

Bob Herger/ Yarrow, Golden Ears Mountains, Fraser valley, British Columbia

George Calef/ Migrating caribou in autumn crossing the Porcupine River downstream from Old Crow, Yukon

Egon Bork/ Rapeseed field and grain elevator, Maidstone, Saskatchewan

Marin Petkov/ Night view of Vancouver from Cypress Bowl Provincial Park

Peter Frank/Lightning storm over Ottawa, Ontario

Tom Knott/ Douglas fir and oaks, Hornby Island, British Columbia

Tom Knott/ Roadside stream in Wells Grey Provincial Park, British Columbia

Brian Milne/Aspen forest along Peace River, near Fort St. John, British Columbia

Tom Knott/Intertidal rock, Hornby Island, British Columbia

Tom Knott/ Spahats Creek Falls at dawn, near Clearwater, British Columbia

Jeremy Addington/ Shore of Moyie Lake, British Columbia

Gregory Horne/ Pre-Cambrian granite, shore of Candlestick Pond, Gros Morne National Park, Newfoundland

George Calef/ Aerial view of glacial erratics and tidal mudflats, Wager Bay, Northwest Territories

Charlie Clayton/ Cold morning from Hillcrest Park, Thunder Bay, Ontario

George Calef/ Spring frost at Marion Lake, Coast Mountains, British Columbia

Brian Milne/Richardson Mountains from the Dempster Highway, Yukon–Northwest Territories boundary

Egon Bork/ Small unnamed glacier viewed from above, near Pipestone Pass, Banff National Park

Victor Killing/ Frost-split glacial erratic, Peggy's Cove, Nova Scotia

Tom Knott/ Split rock and lichens, Monck Provincial Park, British Columbia

Pat Morrow/ Alpine wildflowers on Idaho Mountain, Selkirk Mountains, British Columbia

Freeman Patterson/ Summer mist north of Hunter River, Prince Edward Island

Scott Rowed/ Waterfall and setting moon, the Bugaboos, British Columbia

Frances Cochran/ Olympic Chair at sunrise, Lake Louise, Banff National Park

Egon Bork/ Erosion pattern, Dinosaur Provincial Park, Alberta

Karl Sommerer/ Early snow near Nairn Centre, Ontario

Marin Petkov/ Fog in Central Park, Burnaby, British Columbia

Egon Bork/ Thunderhead west of Elkwater, Cypress Hills region, Alberta

Brent Evans / Cascade Falls on Cascade Mountain, Banff National Park

Richard Vroom/ Canada geese, Eyebrow Lake, Saskatchewan

Chic Harris/ Cirrus cloud, Carberry Sandhills, Spruce Woods Provincial Park, Manitoba

Hans Blohm/ Aspens above the Alaska Highway east of Whitehorse, Yukon

Anders Lenes/ Glacial millhole
below Zillmer Glacier, Cariboo
Mountains, British Columbia

Al Williams / Reeds and reflected sky, Second Vermilion Lake, Banff National Park

Fraser Clark/ Water hyacinth
north of Honey Harbour, Georgian
Bay, Ontario

Chic Harris/ Kennebecasis River near Hampton, New Brunswick

Fraser Clark/ Small cascade beside Shannon Falls near Squamish, British Columbia

Lance W. Camp/ Between storms on Sentinel Peak, northern Selkirk Mountains, British Columbia

Fred Bruemmer/Ice floe near Pond Inlet, southern Baffin Island, Northwest Territories

Egon Bork/ Creek in winter near Banff, Banff National Park

Brian Milne/ Geological camp, Tanquary Fiord, Ellesmere Island, Northwest Territories

Egon Bork / Spring break-up at Beaverhill Lake near Tofield, Alberta

George Calef/ Autumn tundra at tree line near Big Lake, Northwest Territories

Karl Sommerer/ Boathouse and gull near Glen Orchard, Muskoka Lakes region, Ontario

Karl Sommerer/ Alaska Highway after small shower near Haines Junction, Kluane National Park, Yukon

R. D. Muir/ Beaver pond in winter near Ottawa, Ontario

George Calef/ Wind pattern on Big Lake, Northwest Territories

George Calef/ Wave near Tlell, east coast of Graham Island, Queen Charlotte Islands, British Columbia

Tim Fitzharris/ Garry oak, southern Vancouver Island, British Columbia

Tom Yates/ Hayfield and farmhouse, north coast of Prince Edward Island

Egon Bork/ Moose Lake near Jasper, Jasper National Park

Scott Rowed/ Hoarfrost on tree at Vermilion Pass, Kootenay National Park, British Columbia

The Photographers

Jeremy Addington
Paul von Baich
Hans Blohm
Egon Bork
Michel Bourque
Fred Bruemmer
George Calef
Lance W. Camp
Peter Christopher
Vince Claerhout
Fraser Clark
Charlie Clayton
Frances Cochran
Lorne Coulson
Gera Dillon
Brent Evans
Menno Fieguth
Tim Fitzharris
Peter Frank
Paul S. Guyot
Chic Harris

Bob Herger
Gregory Horne
Victor Killing
Tom Knott
Ulrich Kretschmar
Anders Lenes
Norman R. Lightfoot
Gunter Marx
Brian Milne
Pat Morrow
R.D. Muir
Freeman Patterson
Marin Petkov
Scott Rowed
Karl Sommerer
Mark Tomalty
John de Visser
Richard Vroom
Al Williams
Tom Yates
Catherine M. Young

Jeremy Addington *22, 60, 61*

"Currently, I am teaching photography at the David Thompson University Centre in Nelson, British Columbia," writes Jeremy Addington. "Between my home and the school (about fourteen miles) there is a good variety of landscape and it is here that most of my photos are made.

"What I find interesting to photograph changes as much with my mood as it does with the light. It intrigues me that even with a variety of subjects photographed under a variety of conditions and moods, certain attitudes tend to reveal themselves with remarkable consistency.

"Often I am not aware of my attitude. (Moods — excitement, depression, and so on — are, on the contrary, easy to identify.) When I am photographing, I am far more conscious of other things: the light, exposure, the frame, the vantage point. When I make the prints or see the slides I become more aware that my feelings directed the entire enterprise.

"Asking myself what I feel about the land and then trying to express these feelings in photographs limits the possibilities. It is more fruitful for me to first photograph, then ask this question of the photographs. Happily, good photographs respond to the question in a profound way: ineffably."

Paul von Baich *26, 33*

After studying and working in photography in his native Austria, Paul von Baich came to Canada. He immediately fell in love with the northern wilderness, which, unfortunately, did not treat him in kind.

With two friends he set off down the Burntwood River for Hudson Bay. Their boat capsized and all their gear, including von Baich's movie camera, a Leica with valuable lenses, and film, was lost down the rapids. On a later expedition down the turbulent Rivière au Clair in Labrador, von Baich's kayak was smashed and another expensive Leica went down the drain. On the same trip, he and his friends were surprised to be apprehended for trespassing in what ought to have been some of the most deserted country anywhere. Development on the nearby Churchill Falls power project was beginning, and travellers without special permits were suspect.

"We wrecked again," von Baich laughs, describing his first trip to the Yukon. "This time we wrecked our car. We left it on the Klondike Highway, built a raft at Pelly Crossing, packed our gear onto the raft, and travelled down the Yukon River past Dawson and into Alaska. At Eagle, we left the raft and backpacked into the Yukon mountains where we ran out of food."

Despite such rough times, the northern wilderness remains closest to von Baich's heart, although with a half dozen books about various regions to his credit, he hasn't neglected the rest of the country.

"A good photograph has to enchant," he reflects. "An image should affect your emotions, should put you into a mood, and the mood can be manifold."

"I like," he adds, "the surprises that come in photography, the spontaneity of unpredictable situations that occur very suddenly and vanish very suddenly."

Hans Blohm *20, 84, 107*

Driving long distances in a blizzard is an experience Hans Blohm enjoys "tremendously" both for the challenge and for the spectacle it presents. "The heavier it gets, the more fun it is for me," he says. "I can sing into a storm with great gusto. And yet it can, in a moment, fill me with awe and silence. To me, the excitement of photographing the land is found not only in seeing it, but in feeling it, feeling the rain, the sunshine, the heat, the ice crystals in the air at forty below in the Yukon."

Blohm displays an intense, restless enthusiasm for photography and the world it explores. This hasn't been dampened in the least by the daily business of earning a living from it. One of his numerous specialities, making greatly magnified photos of high technology items, maintains a fascination in small things which he has had since he was a child. At the opposite end of the scale, he has done a considerable amount of photography from airplanes. He finds more similarities than differences in his approach to such seemingly disparate subjects.

"I feel the same elation when looking through a microscope as I do when sitting on a mountain top or by the ocean," he says. "It gives me the same sort of excitement. I can envisage displaying microphotographs together with landscape photographs. Deep down, you see the same elements, the same creative forces at work."

Indeed, a number of Blohm's photos of microcircuitry look like aerial views of cities taken by night or by day. Some of his aerial compositions, on the other hand, resemble microscope views of crystals or cell structures.

"It shows to me," he reflects, "the oneness of the universe."

Egon Bork *25, 35, 43, 50, 51, 67, 74, 79, 85, 94, 96, 110, 111*

Michel Bourque *38*

Fred Bruemmer *49, 93*

A fundamental quality of photography is its ability to render its subjects in precise, total detail. A predominant quality of our environment is the random anarchy of its myriad details. The visible world is a busy and messy place; a camera triggered blindly or with lack of skill will not show it to be anything different.

To extract an image of clarity and balance from apparent chaos, while at the same time remaining faithful to the camera's paramount potential for exactness, is the contradiction which challenges those who photograph landscape.

It is a challenge Egon Bork deals with masterfully. All of his landscapes are as sharp in definition as the fine technology of 35mm photography allows. There are rare deliberately-made exceptions, such as some photos of moving water. His work, however, goes far beyond disciplined technique. His self-contained images show idealized landscapes composed of everything that is essential and only that which is essential — nothing less and nothing more.

Particularly intrigued by the prairie and mountain regions of the west, Bork mentions that he often uses telephoto lenses (one of his favourites is the 180mm) to isolate or abstract land forms and landscape patterns. Sometimes he uses exposure to strengthen the lucidity of an image; deliberate underexposure of his photo on page 79 eliminated all detail in the foreground while bringing out the colours in the cloud. Sometimes timing is crucial; in his photo on page 111, the central mountain range, so cleanly separated from both the one in front of and the one behind it, was blanketed by the cloud shadow for only a brief period.

"Canada is still a wild country in most of its range, but in the civilized part man is changing the environment so quickly that many landscape pictures become archival after just a few years," observes Michel Bourque.

A veterinarian by trade, his main interest is wildlife photography. He usually plans his photography for specific subjects, but stays aware of the surroundings and carries a lot of gear in order to be able to meet any situation.

About his photography, Bourque writes, "Having always been involved in nature exploration, I would feel sad without a camera to fix the fragile and menaced wonders it offers to our admiration. The challenge is to go over the plain record and to convey in a finite frame the infinite feeling of these close encounters. Whether it be a tiny insect or a breathtaking landscape, the photographer is privileged to see and feel a dimension most non-photographers are unaware of. Even when we don't carry a camera, this consciousness certainly contributes to the joy of life."

"For me, landscape photography is simply part of an abiding love: to see as much as possible of the Arctic and to record it," writes Fred Bruemmer. "For more than twenty years, the Arctic has been my second home. I spend at least six months of each year there. I photograph the people, plants, and animals, and, of course, the landscape in all its variety and moods. To me, the overwhelming impression of the Arctic is one of infinite space and loneliness, of awesome and austere grandeur, and I try, not always successfully, to convey this feeling in my photographs of northern landscapes.

"Specializing in one field has, I think, a considerable number of personal and material advantages for a photographer. One becomes deeply and ever increasingly involved with one's subject. Each series of pictures that one takes supplements pictures one has taken on previous occasions."

From his extensive collection, Bruemmer has seen many thousands of his photos published. He produces, on the average, about thirty magazine articles a year with the occasional book thrown in for good measure. And, unlike almost every other professional photographer, he works entirely on speculation, almost never on assignment.

"With some luck and a lot of work and perseverance," he concludes, "one can arrive at what is to me the ideal existence: to do what one most enjoys doing and to make an adequate living with it."

115

George Calef   48, 63, 65, 97, 103, 104   Lance W. Camp   29, 92   Peter Christopher   41

Usually the photographers who achieve the most impact on our sensibilities, who contribute the most to our awareness, are those who at some stage concentrated their time, effort, and concern on one subject. For George Calef, that subject has been caribou and the barren-lands with which they are magnificently, primevally interrelated.

"The huge herds are a great, almost geological force on the land," he notes. "The passage of millions of hooves over the centuries has changed the terrain, carving permanent migration trails more than a foot deep in many places. When a herd passes through, a previously desolate place is completely transformed as wolves, foxes, ravens, and other species accompany the caribou. Everything comes to life."

Calef was first attracted to the north not because of its photographic possibilities, but because he wanted to experience the freedom of the wilderness. Having grown up in a big American city, he longed to go "where the animals were still free, where their populations remained largely unaffected by man. At the time, the north was about the only remaining place where this was the case."

A wildlife biologist, Calef has established a reputation as an eloquent communicator with both the camera and the pen. His photographic tastes are enthusiastically unrestrained. "I photograph best and most actively in a new place," he observes. "I prefer strong colours, striking patterns, and I take lots of back-lighted pictures. I am always looking for graphic quality in images, and I like the very strong contrasts and outlined shapes which back-lighting gives."

"Photography has always interested me as a means of recording the extraordinary," writes Lance Camp. "Rather than attempting to take extraordinary photos of mundane objects, I would rather achieve an *adequate* photo of a worthy and dramatic subject. The resulting scene should draw attention to the subject itself rather than the means, techniques, or personality of the photographer.

"This is not easily achieved, however, and requires a great deal of persistence, not to mention luck! To me, a great photo has an overriding simplicity and impact to which all details and complications present in the composition must be subservient. Achieving this effective simplicity is always the hardest thing. Details must be adjusted or eliminated.

"The camera seems, in the end, best suited to the recording of intimate subjects. Subjects of grandeur and great dramatic impact often result in photos akin to looking through a telescope backwards. Grandeur in miniature can result, yes, but usually the resulting photo is an insignificant rendering of the original scene. Yet this grandeur and drama are what appeal to me most strongly, and this is the challenge I like to meet."

Both of Camp's photos shown here admirably pay tribute to the extraordinary. The rainbow on page 92, high in the mountains, is perhaps not so uncommon an occurrence in itself; but the discomfort and danger inherent in climbing peaks during summer storms make it one that is almost never seen, much less recorded, by most photographers. His photo on page 29 was taken at the end of a scorchingly hot day, rare in Alberta, when the extreme heat had given the road surfaces the unusual capability of reflecting the sky.

One of the most imaginative and busiest freelance corporate photographers in the country, Peter Christopher is stimulated by the challenge of tremendous pressure. Assigned narrow, firm deadlines to photograph what are often uninspiring objects — oil rigs, for example — in unflattering settings, he is required "to make them look terrific."

During a season that runs from July to January, he works non-stop seven days a week, fourteen or more hours a day. A typical day begins outdoors before sunrise. Taking advantage of low-angle light, Christopher usually will photograph exteriors until about ten o'clock and again from three until sunset, reserving the less flattering mid-day hours for indoor work.

Unlike many photographers in his field, he doesn't use assistants. "You can't concentrate as well, and you have to worry about when to feed them," he explains. "In this business, there are no such things as coffee breaks, lunches, or dinners."

Although he estimates eighty per cent of his work is done with only two lenses, a 24mm and an 85mm, he must be prepared for any eventuality and so takes some two hundred pounds of photographic equipment on every assignment. So that he can move around without an assistant, all this gear is fitted into a custom-made case on wheels which also has room for fifty pounds of his personal luggage.

To get a different angle on subjects, Christopher often does aerial photography, generally preferring fixed-wing craft over helicopters, and flying quite low to eliminate the effect of haze while using wide-angle lenses, 24mm or 28mm, to preserve the feeling of altitude.

Vince Claerhout *39*

Formally trained in natural history and education, Vince Claerhout is self-taught in photography and lists the outdoors, his natural history background, and the works of other photographers as his main sources of inspiration.

"I take pictures in order to gain from the experience, to capture a moment, an insight into the phenomena of life which can be relived at every showing," he writes. "It is my hope that any viewer of my work may become an active participant in the experience and share some of the exhilaration that I feel."

His photo on page 39 was taken near where he lives in southwestern Alberta. "The Pincher Creek region is an intriguing place in which to live and photograph," he maintains. "The plains butt up to the mountains, creating unique weather patterns. Plant growth in unprotected areas is stunted and contorted due to the gnarling bite of the wind. Water and wind erosion is prevalent. Dramatic cloud formations commonly accompany rapidly changing weather. Warm chinook winds can melt a couple of feet of snow within hours. Dust will be flying from the roadways in mid-January while several feet of snow lies in the fields. At times, literally a lapse of a second can mean the difference between the fixing of a dramatic moment on film or merely in one's mind."

Fraser Clark *89, 91*

There are two basic ways to approach landscape photography. One is to be as empty of preconceptions and preferences as possible; to treat each photograph as unique and distinct from others one has made; to allow each subject, each opportunity to inspire the particular fashion in which it is to be photographed. The other is to impose a consistent, particular way of seeing onto one's photograph, choosing subject and viewpoint to conform to a predetermined style.

Fraser Clark prefers the second approach. "I like to look for blocks of colour and shapes that interact on a plane to form simple, pleasing geometrics," he says. "I look for geometrics and graphics in the landscape, that's what draws my eye to a potential photograph. I also prefer photographs that transcend what they are pictures of and suggest something else at the same time."

His photo on page 89 he calls *Calligraphy*, as it suggests elaborate script. Clark uses colour, form, and light as basically equivalent and interchangeable blocks in his compositions. His picture on page 91 serves as a good example; the *shape* of the lit areas was of primary importance to him rather than any quality or mood in the light.

"As opposed to some photographers who let nature flow through them, I go out there and try to impose my own intellect, my own mind onto nature," he explains. "I am trying to formulate something out of nature that appeals to my own vision."

His statement intends no value judgement. As a partner in a prestigious Toronto photo gallery, he says, "I love photography in general, I love all kinds of it. That is why I am in the business. And I am very fortunate in that I get to see a lot of it."

Charlie Clayton *24, 64*

"A little bit of work and a lot of love," is how Charlie Clayton describes his approach to photography. Subjects which interest him include "anything that's great," which for someone with his bright enthusiasm, turns out to be just about everything. "There is so much in the world to get excited about," he adds.

To ensure that he doesn't miss any of it, he always keeps his cameras ready in his car, and is always eager to rush off to a fire or other extraordinary event.

His habit of preparedness once saved the life of a moose. Taking short leave of his job at the grain commission in Thunder Bay when he heard that the wild animal had been spotted in a city park, he arrived on the scene to find the police preparing to shoot it. An argument ensued. Clayton, lobbying for support from numerous bystanders, threatened to tell as many people as he could that the moose would be needlessly killed. Armed with his cameras, it was evident that he meant business. The police brought in an expert with a tranquilizer gun and the moose, doped but alive, was trucked off back to the wilderness.

Always having his cameras in his car allowed Clayton the picture on page 65, which he made one bitterly cold morning on his way to work.

Although he has travelled across the country, his favourite place for photography is Cape Sibley, close to his home in Thunder Bay. "It is like a forgotten place," he explains, "but there are some great things there, like little jewels. I remember a time when an ice storm coated all the rocks and trees. It was like a magic land. But it is not usually like icing on a cake — you have to look hard for your photographs."

Frances Cochran 73

"Down in the valley it was grey and miserable, and all of a sudden you came out into Shangri-La," says Frances Cochran, describing the experience which led up to her photo on page 73.

Working on a story about avalanche control, she had followed the ski patrol up the chair lift, deserted before official opening time. The day looked unpromising when unexpectedly she rode through the clouds just as dawn was breaking over the mountain tops.

Cochran, who comes from an artistic family, had her first serious encounter with photography while taking a graphic design course at art school. "The first camera I ever learned from was a 4" x 5", she remembers. "We were taught about apertures and shutter speeds with nude models all over the studio."

Notwithstanding her subsequent formal study in photography at the Banff Centre, Cochran feels she learned by far the most about her chosen specialty when she worked as a freelance press photographer. "I learned about working quickly and getting it right the first time," she notes.

An accomplished skier with a passion for the outdoors, she loves cold weather. "It's crisp, it's invigorating, it preserves me.

"I like snow," she continues. "I like how it defines certain things, how it softens other things. I like travelling in it, the adventure of it. I like storms. I like what a snowstorm can do to a building or a tree, daubing it in the manner of an impressionist painting. I like what happens to light when it goes through snow. It's clean. I like white."

Lorne Coulson 46

"Much of my work features the Manitoba landscape because of its accessibility and familiarity, as well as its wide diversity of subtle, beautiful subject matter," writes Lorne Coulson, who lives in Winnipeg.

His photo on page 46 is an example of the perhaps unexpected kind of beauty to be discovered in his province. A unique area with sand dunes and cacti, the Carberry Sandhills are, unfortunately, subject to erosion from heavy artillery and tank practice.

"At the time this photograph was taken," Coulson points out, "a person entered the area in spite of ominous military signs warning of dire consequences. Now, a single square mile has been officially set off, and designated paths requiring tour guides are the only permitted means of entry into the area. But you can still hear the bombs explode and see Leopard tanks churning up the dunes in the distance."

To add interest to the day, Coulson had borrowed a 21mm lens, which has since become one of his favourites. "This lens echoes and emphasizes our non-ending stretch of prairie landscape and forces one to get into close contact with the subject matter at hand," he explains.

"My decision to photograph is done on an intuitive basis. I know when I have come upon a scene that will record on film in an exciting manner. This can take place in the form of some combination of simple design, colour, lighting. The rest involves a particular lens, viewpoint, and not making any technical mistakes. In this manner, photography provides me with a medium to explore, contemplate, and discover my world. If any of my photographs bring out in others the excitement and sentiment that I feel, then this activity becomes very satisfying and meaningful to me."

Gera Dillon 17, 21, 32

"I don't think most photographers consider themselves as conforming to a particular 'style,'" observes Gera Dillon. "I call myself an 'imagist-at-large'; I feel that there is so much imagery out there that I should be open to it all. A photographer has to be flexible in his approach."

Dillon finds that his approach to photography is often impressionistic, in the sense of being concerned with that which is changing, elusive, short-lived. Referring to his photo on page 17 by way of example, he says, "That kind of rare image much more often comes by chance rather than by premeditation. Because of that very momentary aspect, some conjunction of light in the right circumstances, you have a feeling that things aren't going to be like that again, that it is a once-in-a-lifetime moment. Something that is very fleeting, that doesn't linger long, I find the most satisfying. To capture it properly, you have to have what I call 'practiced spontaneity.' The most successful shots, I find, are the ones where you feel an anxiety — you have to get it *fast*."

For Dillon, photography is the extracting of essentials, the finding of the part which best represents the whole. "All landscapes," he points out, "are details of a much larger thing. It can be a vast prairie scene photographed with a wide-angle lens, but it is still only a detail of everything that is there. The main task of the photographer is to extract from the whole environment that detail which epitomizes, which says it all. Whether a landscape photograph is great or merely good depends on how well it has extracted from the grand scale the optimum image which speaks for the larger context."

Brent Evans *80*

"I have been told several times that many of my photographs require the viewer to get within nose-touching distance," mentions Brent Evans. Indeed, that is an apt observation for more than one reason.

Evans, whose favourite landscapes are sea coasts, deserts, and "big rock places," portrays unassumingly real places in an almost artless manner. This gives his pictures a quality that seems to invite the viewer to casually step into his scenes, rather than to hold them at arm's length and admire them as great photographs. There is seldom anything obviously extraordinary about the lighting, subject matter, or viewpoint taken. His work is subtle, but not in the ways in which we usually think of photos as being subtle, such as subdued monochromatic colour or delicate lines and textures. In fact, on cursory viewing, one might be tempted to pass off some of his pictures as mere records or snapshots. Unlike snapshots, however, these never become boring, and possess a staying power over the course of many viewings that is almost inexplicable.

Closer scrutiny of Evans's pictures, moreover, often reveals some initially unnoticed special characteristic, such as very strong composition hidden beneath inherently unordered subject matter. At first glance, his photo on page 80 appears to be of a relatively small waterfall, close to the background in the upper right. However, the background turns out to be far away, a forest in the valley below. The difference between the actual scale and the illusory scale creates a surprise and tension which prompts close study and sustains interest.

Menno Fieguth *34*

"The best pictures you get are taken where you live," believes Menno Fieguth. "It has to do with understanding the terrain. To put it more bluntly, if you can't take good photos in your backyard, you won't be able to take good photos anywhere else either. A useful exercise would be to take one roll of film, one lens, and spend one day along a one-mile section of road near your home to see what you can come up with."

Fieguth, who lives in Saskatchewan, has especially alerted people to the beauty of the prairies, but as an accomplished professional, he takes good photographs wherever he goes. He has discovered that he favours different lenses for different parts of the country: on the prairies, he often settles for his 80-200mm zoom or his 300mm; he might work all day in the mountains with just a 24mm or a 35mm; and on Vancouver Island, he found that he used his 16mm much more often than usual.

Concerning his approach to photography, Fieguth says, "I feel I have the obligation to subordinate myself to the subject; not to express myself. No personality, no personality problem."

One of his most memorable assignments saw Fieguth return home dressed only in his pyjamas after the motel in which he was staying burned down — with his clothes and cameras in it.

Tim Fitzharris *87, 106*

"I follow my nose," writes Tim Fitzharris, commenting on how he searches for pictures. "My orientation is toward real things rather than concepts or approaches. I get excited by something that I see, or think that I see, and then I try to figure out how I can show it without losing anything. I tend towards the romantic with most subjects. Birds still get me more excited than anything else. I am grateful that there is something that gets me excited."

It is worth noting that Fitzharris ranks among the very best of bird photographers. When it comes to landscape photography, he has always thought of the term "as rather an archaic expression, suggestive of accepted, traditional approaches." It is the image, not its pigeon-holed category, that counts. Few people, he points out, would think of his photo on page 87 as a landscape, since it lacks both land and perspective, two elements expected of the stereotype "landscape."

A successful photograph, he feels, "has to be exciting to look at in a strictly graphic sense, has to be original, unique in concept, and has to be free of technical compromises or compositional flaws."

Concerning the Canadian landscape, he writes, "What impresses me is the spaciousness, the wonderful feeling of living on the edge of the crowd of humanity and being able to get away from it at any time simply by driving north for a few hours. I especially like the prairies — empty, dry, great skies, nostalgia, romance, and a view that never stops. I live on Vancouver Island now, which gives me the luxury of both a northern edge and a western edge, in effect a corner lot with lots of freedom and space."

Peter Frank *53*

The popular idea of "landscape" is a scene, out there waiting, ready to be snapped by anyone coming across it after, say, a leisurely drive in the country. But the landscape changes continually; and from the point of view of the photographer, for whom light is of critical concern, the landscape is constantly on the move. If one waits long enough in one place, the opportunity to photograph a dramatic landscape will someday arrive, even perhaps at one's own doorstep. Peter Frank made his photo on page 53 from his living room.

Nature's equivalent of electronic flash, a lightning strike is usually briefer in duration than the reaction time of human reflexes. Hence lightning must be literally left to photograph itself. Frank describes how he made the photo: "This is a view from my apartment. I saw the storm coming, set up my camera and tripod, and shot through an open window. I framed the picture the way I wanted it and then hoped that lightning would strike within the area framed. The shutter was set at 'B' and the diaphragm stopped down to allow a long exposure. Then I waited and watched. When one or two lightning bolts struck within the framed area, I closed the shutter. If no lightning struck within five to seven minutes, I closed the shutter and started exposing a new frame."

Frank works for the Museum of Natural Sciences. Of his photography, he writes: "I concentrate mostly on nature and landscape and use 35mm and 2" x 2" format. While the versatility and compactness of the 35mm system is a great advantage, I find I sometimes tend to shoot a lot and hope for a good picture. The larger format forces me to slow down and study a scene carefully before making an exposure."

Paul S. Guyot *18*

Paul Guyot is one of those enviable people destined to remain forever young. After twenty-five years of travel across Canada as a CBC cameraman, he retains an exuberant wonder and enthusiasm for the natural beauty of the land. He thinks nothing of rising at 4:00 A.M. just to watch and listen to migrating geese — something he has done on countless occasions. "I can never overcome that childlike excitement when I am confronted by a beautiful scene," he admits unabashedly.

He particularly adores canoe country, his favourite choice for photography. He describes how he made his photo on page 18: "Returning home from a canoe trip in Quetico Park one autumn, we stayed overnight at a lodge on Nym Lake. The following day, I was awake at 4:00 A.M. The lake, still as glass, was beckoning. In my canoe, I slipped quietly into the eerie light of the lake, not to discover its mysteries, but to be in communion with the dawn, the overture to the coming day.

"As darkness slowly dissipated, this small islet came into view. To the north, along the far shoreline, a bank of fog was moving slowly southward. I waited a good half hour, hoping for the background to be shrouded in mist as the sun rose. My anticipation paid off. A slight canoe adjustment and I recorded what I call *A New Day Is Born* in a spectacular display of light and tranquillity in the wilderness."

Chick Harris *42, 83, 90*

"Keep your eyes open, good things to photograph are everywhere," advises Chic Harris. Not one to take such an apparently obvious idea for granted, he recently shot some eighty rolls of film on his patio and in his backyard, surprising even himself with how much he could find in the kind of setting most of us don't normally look at too carefully.

Harris finds that, more and more, he is concerned with compositional studies rather than the literal documentation of nature which used to be his main interest. He might, for example, photograph the reflection on his toaster, deliberately throwing the picture out of focus to turn it into a design purely of colour and shape.

Fine art is one source of inspiration for him, and he has no qualms about allowing a particular painting to inspire his photographs. "When you paint, you are expected to stimulate others," he notes. Nor does he worry about originality, observing that, "The more you look at exhibits and publications, the more you find that other people have caught on to the same ideas."

Harris prefers to be able to take his time on his landscapes, but this is not always possible. Sometimes fast-breaking conditions necessitate a "grab shot." His photo on page 83 is case in point. "I had to race up the sand dune," he remembers. "The cloud was moving at tremendous speed. I was only able to get one photograph like this before it was too late."

For Harris, a successful picture "is one that holds your eye within the picture frame," and for successful photography "it is important to be willing to get up early in the morning."

Bob Herger *44, 47, 105*

"I don't photograph only for myself, I photograph for my children and their children," explains Bob Herger, acutely aware of the potential of photography to preserve something of spiritual value.

He lives in the Fraser valley of British Columbia, an area facing intense development pressure. The scene on page 47, he points out, was destined to become a municipal garbage dump until vociferous local opinion stopped the plan, perhaps only temporarily. "One day, the whole valley will be one large Vancouver," he laments.

When it comes to landscapes, Herger is the quintessential perfectionist. He will not photograph a scene unless it will turn out exactly the way he wants it; he will return again and again to the same place until everything is just right. His photo on page 44, taken around 4:30 A.M., was made after he had left home in the dark for the third time to drive the long distance to the same spot. That was actually a relatively easy picture for Herger. His photo on page 47 was taken on the twenty-second trip to the location over a two-year period. The picture represents the first and only time he actually used his film at the spot. On every other occasion the light or some other condition wasn't precisely the way he had envisaged it, so he did not bother photographing.

Herger's uncompromising approach is all the more remarkable in light of the fact that he manages a stock photography agency, a business where quantity of choice often means greater success that quality. Dedicated to high standards in the industry, Herger also serves as an editor and consultant on photography for several major publishing firms, and has produced books of his own work.

Gregory Horne *62*

The mountains are Gregory Horne's favourite location for photography, and he is particularly fascinated by natural textures and patterns. "I am always surveying the environment for these features, whether they be several centimeters or several kilometers in scope," he mentions.

His photo on page 62, he writes, "was made on the shore of a pond situated in a glacial scoured basin on the plateau-like Long Range Mountains. These mountains are predominantly of Pre-Cambrian granite, and, like the Canadian Shield, are at least 600 million years old. The glassy calm early morning water makes the lichen-decorated rock appear to be floating in an inky space. A polarizing filter was used to bring out this effect."

The photograph is an excellent illustration of the fact that the merits of landscape photography have little to do with scale. Through mood and simplicity the picture imparts to its subject a monumental quality that is often missing from photographs of landscapes on a much grander scale. In addition, the photo is a quintessentially Canadian scene. In its basic statement of stone and water, it is evocative of the essential character of the land.

Horne works as a park warden in Jasper National Park. "Photography is a way of preserving and conveying the images I see and appreciate in nature. I enjoy giving slide show lectures using my work. Idealistically, I hope that something will have rubbed off on the audience. Maybe the next time they see a similar scene, their esteem for nature will be higher."

Victor Killing *68*

For the sake of rich variety, each photograph in a book of this kind is chosen on its own distinctive merits but is necessarily judged against others similar in treatment and subject. This puts limits on reproducing the cumulative effect of a photographer's work where numerous images constitute an in-depth study of one type of subject.

Victor Killing's photo on page 68 is part of such a study. He returned twice to the Atlantic coast of Nova Scotia simply to photograph boulders.

Killing became engrossed in the boulders because of their sculptural qualities, and his pictures convey something of the primeval essence of a place which has become better known for the picturesqueness of its man-made aspects. In addition, many of his boulder pictures explore a relationship between negative and positive shapes; the blank sky between and behind the rocks having a shape all its own.

He hopes to do another series on rocks, this time examining those around Georgian Bay, which he finds are much different — smoother and more polished — than those he examined around Peggy's Cove.

Killing doesn't limit his photography to boulders. Inspired in the 1930s by the landscape work of Weston, Strand, and Adams, he studied photography in New York. He photographed women's fashions for a while before deciding it wasn't what he wanted to do and turning to a career in architectural drafting, design, and teaching.

"My photography is a response to the love and awe I have for the natural scene," he sums up. "Basically, I work to please myself."

Tom Knott

Of his involvement with photography, which consists of making 8" x 10" black-and-white contact prints of landscapes, Tom Knott writes, "The first couple of years I spent learning technique and taking pictures of everything around, until I began to discover that the quest I was on was finding its most satisfactory expression in images which reached places behind or beyond the everyday awareness of the world; images which evoked several levels of emotion and understanding at once or in sequence. It is not very easy to define this quest I am on, not in words. I can say that it has to do with understanding the laws of the universe that underlie its physical aspect. I suspect that this is fundamentally a spiritual quest.

"For me, the act of photographing something serves as a bridge between appearance and essence, and, by carrying off something from that place between worlds, I can deepen my own understanding and also, very importantly, begin to communicate with others.

"That process of communication by images is one which gives me a lot of pleasure. Images are non-rational, non-linear, multi-levelled, complex things. I am always delighted when someone discovers something in or through one of my photographs that I had not recognized in it. This to me is a sign of success, because I believe that the place where these images are made is inexhaustibly deep and rich.

"When I am photographing, my conscious mind is usually very quiet, with just enough ego functioning to keep the photographer physically intact, and just enough intellect to get the exposure right. For the rest, I am a wanderer."

Ulrich Kretschmar

"The source of any creativity I may have lies in classical music, nature, physical well-being, and art," writes Ulrich Kretschmar. "I respond instantaneously to situations I encounter in nature, but I also anticipate them to some extent. Art must arise from one's own experience and therefore I try to prospect my own and the collective past."

Among the main influences on his way of seeing, he lists several well-known photographers and Beethoven's late string quartets. His letterhead, which provokes a double-take, contains an acknowledgement and reminder of another influence, essential to all photographers. It reads "Ulrich Kretschmar & Sun, Photographers."

Kretschmar's early years were perhaps more traumatic than most. "It was lucky for me that the only direct hit our house in Dresden received during the attack in 1945 was a dud. I was only three at the time, but I still recollect burning phosphorus dripping from the eaves as we fled through the burning city."

Kretschmar today maintains an intense involvement in several fields, including playing classical flute and cross-country ski racing as well as developing his numerous ideas in photography. He and his wife are professional geologists.

"In my career, geology and photography are symbiotically related," he concludes. "Both require acute powers of observation, to which photos attest. It is in part through geological knowledge that my photos gain any substance they may have. On the other hand, a geological background is also a hindrance, since it is the task of the scientist to demystify. The artist's task, however, is diametrically opposed. Attempts to resolve this dilemma will always constitute a challenge and be a source of creativity."

Anders Lenes

Despite the often made (and often inappropriate) comparison between painting and photography, there are in fact very few people who work in both mediums. Anders Lenes is a rare exception. He makes surreal expressionistic paintings as large as six by eight feet. In photography, he works in several formats ranging from 35mm to 8" x 10".

Of his two interests, he says, "The two don't relate. They are totally different. For me, photography is for capturing beauty; it helps me to see better. Painting is for self-expression; it is psychologically draining. I don't paint naturalistic scenes — I would rather take a photograph. I can't say that one is more important than the other, although one might be more important at a particular time."

Based in Banff, Lenes also works as a guide with a company that takes hikers into prime alpine regions by helicopter. Part of his task is to instruct interested clients in the basics of photography.

Helicopter access helped Lenes get his rare photo on page 86: it would have taken three or four days to walk into the location. Adding to the remoteness of this beautiful detail was the fact that it was found partway up a smooth rock face and to reach it Lenes made use of his mountain-climbing skills.

Norman R. Lightfoot 27

Primarily a film-maker, Norman Lightfoot has made many excellent documentaries dealing with Canadian artists and with wildlife. Characteristically, the subjects of many of his wildlife films, for example, rodents and reptiles, are often neglected because of their small size and commonness. This concern for the overlooked rather than the conspicuous is just as manifest in his still photography of landscapes.

"There is a whole new world down there that most of us simply walk over," he says. "You may think you know what is there, but you don't until you start looking. You can spend hours on small things within only ten square feet of space. The mini-environment can be just as grand as miles of spacious scenery. It is a matter of getting down on your hands and knees."

Taken with the camera only two feet off the ground on a tripod, his photo on page 27 resulted from such close observation of seemingly inconsequential things, in this case the wake of a boat across still waters. The picture is also, as he points out, a good example of the fact that "so much of photography is nothing more than light, which involves not just the nature of the light source, but the reflecting quality of surfaces."

It is worth noting that, although the picture encompasses a small area, it is nonetheless a recognizably *Canadian* landscape; the characteristic processes and features of the land are continuous and discernible even at this small scale. Lightfoot has spent most of his life in Africa, and he points out that simply the *blueness* of the water, its quality on a subtle level, is not something you would readily find in Africa — or in most other places.

Gunter Marx 37

"The scene struck my eyes while I was driving along the Trans-Canada Highway through the Fraser valley, British Columbia's prime farmland," writes Gunter Marx about his photo on page 37. "Nothing could prevent me from stopping my vehicle and letting my camera have a look at these lines and colours, which turned out to be a tulip field, a little bit of Holland."

Like many photographs of strong impact, this one is effective not only because of its striking composition and colours, but because it challenges our normal assumptions about the reality from which it has been extracted. It is surprising as an authentic Canadian scene; in Holland, a similar picture would perhaps not be perceived as quite as unusual an image.

The picture does, in fact, represent a rare opportunity. The tulip farm in question, the only one of its size in British Columbia, has been in operation for but two years. Moreover, its peak colour lasts no more than a day, since the tulips are cut as soon as they blossom.

Marx is a cabinet maker by trade, but is intensely involved in amateur photography, often giving sophisticated multi-projector slide shows to camera clubs. In addition to landscape and nature, he most enjoys action photography while hiking, cross-country skiing, sailing, or scuba diving.

Brian Milne 56, 66, 95

"I like the pure line of the land, where you can see the land," says Brian Milne. "I like places without any trees. The problem with most of the Canadian landscape is that there are too many trees in the way. I like to photograph from planes and helicopters, it gets me away from the trees."

The photo on page 56 is indeed correctly credited to Milne. It was part of a project of photographing trees, of coming to terms with an unavoidable part of the land.

There is no doubt, however, that Milne's favourite regions are the open spaces of the prairies and the north. He has driven the Alaska Highway seven times each way in the course of his trips to the Yukon and Alaska. All his experiences there, however, didn't prepare him for his first encounter with the high Arctic. "I had never confronted such isolation and barrenness," he admits. "It was so stark. It was a surprise to me; I expected more than I saw when I got there and I had more on film than I thought I had when I returned."

"When there is no wind," he continues, "the high Arctic must have the quietest places in the world. I remember being camped on Ellesmere Island when I heard a distant drone. The sound grew louder and louder, and I expected to see a low-flying aircraft come up over the horizon. It turned out it was a bumble bee."

Earning a living from freelance editorial photography, Milne observes, "is not the great life of carefree travel and wilderness living one might expect. It is only ten per cent photography and ninety per cent marketing. There is a lot of frustration and pressure; the high moments don't last long enough."

Pat Morrow 36, 70

"Be there!" is Pat Morrow's succinct, complete counsel for aspiring freelancers.

Consistent with his own advice, he has been to many difficult to reach, rarely seen places in his world-wide quest for adventure. He has stood on the summits of the highest mountains in both North America (McKinley) and South America (Aconcagua). Recently, while in training for an assault on the world's loftiest mountain as a member of the Canadian Mount Everest Expedition, he reached a higher altitude on cross-country skis than has any other person when he ascended Muztagh Ata, a 7546-meter peak in the Pamirs of central Asia.

Life and photography are "a continuous chain of happy coincidences" for Morrow, who is one of the busiest magazine photographers in the country. Constantly on the move, he has documented stories wide-ranging in their diversity: the quiet trials of family life in the Yukon wilderness; the zany celebrations of Carnaval in Rio; the colourful excitement of the World Hang-Gliding Championships in the Austrian Alps; the preparations of two kamikaze skiers who wanted to descend the precipitous face of the highest mountain in the Canadian Rockies; the masterful craftsmanship of a talented boatbuilder on the British Columbia coast; the unreal beauty of skiing huge sand dunes in remote western China.

In his photojournalistic work as well as in his landscapes, Morrow exhibits a frequent strong use of wide-angle lenses, as is evident from his photos on pages 70 and 36. It has become almost a trademark for the man who takes in as much of life as he can and likes to get as close as possible to where the action is.

R.D. Muir 102

Commenting on what the landscape and photography mean to him, Dalton Muir writes: "An esteemed former teacher (now departed) once said, 'A wild thing must know its environment with indecent familiarity, just to survive.' For me, that knowledge means more than survival; it is enjoyable, motivational, and addictive. Whether it is the euphoric sweep of a glacier-studded Arctic, an active volcano, a profound cave, or the texture of pond ice underfoot, the experiences are synergistic and cumulative.

"There is a reward for walking where no one else has trod. Another comes from perceiving and recording familiar landscapes in a way that no one else has done before. Serious painters and photographers know the feeling. They are personal values, and they may change with time.

"Not everyone cares for landscapes, for certain kinds of landscapes, or for landscapes devoid of people. But I do. Landscapes are an ultimate process, changing, progressing; the only form of evolution that we can directly perceive. The evidence lies on all sides, and from the experience of landscape comes appreciation of time and place, and by derivation, other concepts.

"The transparently thin image layer of a good photograph contains high information density, rivalling that of modern electronic arrays and perhaps comparable to some lower order functions of the brain itself. Small wonder that carefully prepared landscape photographs convey information, experience, and perception to generations beyond the lives of individuals or of existing storage and retrieval systems.

"We make landscape photographs from visual experiences that we value. Landscape images are the celebration of our world, as we encounter it and pass it on."

Freeman Patterson 40, 71, 99

"When it comes to photographing the domestic landscape, as opposed to wilderness, I find that I usually make far more ordered compositions," observes Freeman Patterson, referring to his photos on pages 71 and 99. "This is partly because farmland, or any other land organized by human beings, tends to reflect a certain kind of order, depending on the land use. The reason these compositions are the way they are also relates to my own life becoming more ordered as I get older. More and more I regard messiness as a waste of time, so I keep the top of my desk clean, and I am more conscious of that kind of thing now than I was, say, ten years ago. Thus, because of my own personal development, I have a natural attraction for land that shows the same kind of order. It is reflected in these pictures in minimal subject matter and strong lines."

Referring to his photo on page 40, he says, "the morning mist and the backlighting are restraining the colour tremendously. This is something I really like. Very few of the pictures that I like contain truly striking colour; my overall preference is for this sort of restrained colour."

Few photographers analyse their own work as thoroughly as does Patterson, and few photographers have as much control over their medium. He advises that training in visual design as well as in technical skills is essential to freeing the photographer for spontaneous work.

Among the very best practitioners of photography, he is also one of its most generous and capable teachers. No less than half a dozen of the other photographers in this book acknowledged him as one of their most important influences.

Marin Petkov *52, 77*

Scott Rowed *72, 112*

Karl Sommerer *76, 98, 100, 101*

"Photography for me is a big joy," says Marin Petkov. "Although it is only a hobby, I am very much devoted to it. I first started taking interest in photography about twelve years ago, while travelling through several countries around the world, and it has since become a thrilling part of my life."

The Canadian landscape has become one of his favourite subjects, and he believes that preserving a scene as simply as possible gives the picture more impact and natural beauty.

His photo on page 52 is a case in point. Rather than take the standard calendar picture of the downtown skyline of Vancouver reflected in the harbour, Petkov has captured a more abstract and universal view, a sea of stars. It is a photograph of "the magic of the city at night, of countless lights that taper away quietly into the endless darkness."

His black-and-white photo on page 77 catches fog at the elusive right time in the right place; it sifts the shapes at different distances into progressively lighter tones of grey. For him, it "mirrors a stillness and serenity, a peaceful and quiet moment which can only be captured at one solitary instance, never to be repeated the same way again."

"Being in the right place at the right time comes more from planning and effort than from luck," believes Scott Rowed.

His photo on page 72 is theory put into practice. Rowed had hiked into the rugged Bugaboos, a striking mountain region with which he was already familiar, solely in order to photograph during the full moon. Reversing the usual routine for a photographer, he made pictures at night and slept by day.

On the first night, he camped on a narrow pass high above timber line, surrounded by great dark spires, overlooking a grand icefield that shimmered in the moonlight. Superfluous to say, it was a beautiful experience. The next night, remaining where he was, he got more than he bargained for when a thunderstorm moved in on his exposed site. "It was incredibly violent; I have never heard lightning so close, and the wind nearly flattened my tent," he remembers.

On the third night, he descended to a lower altitude and got this picture an hour before dawn, with the scant light from the approaching day helping to reveal detail in the landscape.

Born in Jasper, Rowed has been hiking, climbing, and ski-mountaineering in the mountains for most of his life. Organizing most of his trips around photography, he often travels solo, companions patient enough to accompany photographers being hard to find.

In addition to freelancing as a photographer, Rowed works as a helicopter skiing guide, finding a satisfying parallel between the two vocations beyond the fact that he does a lot of ski photography. "Both enable me to share the beauty of the mountains with other people," he says.

While Sommerer cannot remember a time when he was not interested in photography, he will never forget the most foolish thing he ever did to get a picture. Just after spring break-up in northern Ontario one year, he set off with his son to canoe and photograph new territory.

"We found a terrific spot where the otherwise slow-moving Bowland River cascaded in a series of rapids and falls into a small lake below," he writes. "An ideal place for a dramatic shot. I put Junior ashore with detailed instructions to photograph me paddling the red canoe near the brink of the falls. 'Take an extra shot should I go over,' I jokingly added.

"You guessed it, over I went. My son got the shot, but showing only the canoe while I was already sucked under. Miraculously I was thrown against a huge rock in the centre of the falls, just before the worst drop over jagged boulders. Canoe, food, camping gear, Rollei, Leicas, lenses were gone. After spending a miserable, frosty night without jackets or fire, we walked out the next day, I barefoot, ten miles through snow, bush, and rocks."

A professional photographer as well as a teacher and lecturer on the subject, Sommerer is equally at home with black-and-white or colour, but finds it difficult to pursue both simultaneously because each demands such a different approach. As a measure of the relative seriousness of his approach to black-and-white work, he notes that he always uses his larger cameras (he owns twenty-eight different models) for such work, and generally reserves the 35mm format for colour.

Mark Tomalty *23*

Photographs compete for our attention in many ways. Mark Tomalty's photo on page 23 is effective for its subtle invitation to a double-take. At first glance, it is a straight-forward picture. Our eye catches the centre of interest, a small waterfall recorded with the familiar silky-smoothness achieved with slow shutter speed. But when we grasp the other elements in the picture we realize an illusion has been created; the main features of the scene seem to be built on two different scales. Either the autumn litter consists of giant leaves or, as we must conclude, the flowing water is not really a waterfall but a tiny trickle no more substantial than that from a small faucet. The illusion here is exactly opposite to that achieved by Brent Evans's photo on page 80.

Like many photographers, Tomalty has had no formal training in photography. However, he considers himself fortunate to have been able to learn by working in a large commercial studio in Montreal. "But," he says, "I still feel I appreciate outdoor photography above anything else."

Among his most memorable experiences as a photographer he lists climbing alone to a blind beside a nest of aggressive goshawks, getting pelted by peppers in a small Mexican market, and being chased from a liquid air plant by two burly employees on motorcycles.

John de Visser *19, 30, 45, 81*

Possibly no other photographer has trav-elled and photographed Canada quite so extensively as has John de Visser. Winter has thus been an unavoidable, and often welcome, fact of life for him. With refer-ence to his photo on page 30, he writes, "I like those winter days when the sky is uniformly cloudy, ideally when it is the same colour as the land, but good enough when it is like this. It makes the landscape more abstract by taking away the depth dimension which shadows give it. As well, in this kind of light, the simpler the compo-nents of the picture, the better they express the lonely emptiness of the winter season on the land."

It is typical of de Visser that, when asked to comment in general on his own work, he defers to his subject: "The Canadian land-scape appeals to me because of its abso-lutely incredible variety but even more because of its size, its scope. This may be the result of having been born in the Neth-erlands, a very small country, about the size of Lake Ontario, and overpopulated to the point of giving me instant claustrophobia when I am there. Here, whether it be on the shore of one of the oceans, in the Canadian Shield of Quebec and Ontario, on the prai-ries, in the mountains, or on the tundra of the North, I feel that I get a better, perhaps the only proper sense of perspective on the insignificance of man in nature, in creation. That may sound pompous. Maybe it is. But having had the very good fortune of spending a lot of time in every part of this country, that's the way I feel."

Richard Vroom *28, 82*

Few photographers have been able to use their career as a passport as much as has Richard Vroom. His cameras have taken him to Japan for the National Film Board, the Caribbean for Air Canada, eastern Europe for *Time* magazine, British Guyana for the Canadian government. He has photographed for the governments of Portugal, Italy, the Philippines, and the Netherlands. For a year, he based himself in Europe and freelanced out of Geneva. Alto-gether, he has worked in more than forty countries on assignment.

In spite of having travelled to so many exotic lands, Vroom considers the most memorable places he has visited to be the north shore of Lake Superior, Baffin Island, and the Rockies. "Throughout Canada, there is more that is untouched, untapped right at one's back doorstep," he points out. "There is a greater variation in the seasons here than in any other country."

Vroom's great interest is showing the heritage of Canada to others. At present, he is in charge of still photography at the Department of External Affairs, a responsi-bility that has reversed his role in the profession. He now purchases photographs and sends other photographers out on assignments. "I miss the freedom of free-lancing, the adventure trips, seeing new places first hand, getting involved with different cultures," he says. "But on the other hand, I enjoy the rewards that go with producing exhibitions and publications."

Al Williams *31, 57, 88*　　　　**Tom Yates** *108, 109*　　　　**Catherine M. Young** *75*

"I look for light, rather than a landscape," says Al Williams, emphasizing his priorities. Such conscious preference for the elusive over the permanent can lead to frustration, but, as he points out, one might capture a moment that may never happen again. The dramatic lighting which created the strong contrasts in his picture on page 31, lasted no more than a couple of minutes.

"Occasionally I put myself in a potentially beautiful landscape and wait for the right moment," he adds. The ethereal mood of his photo on page 88 belies the perseverance invested in its making: several long hours of patient waiting on a mosquito-infested shore for the clouds to move into just the right position. The strong image Williams thus extracted from a group of normally nondescript reeds indicates his well-practiced ability to previsualize and plan.

"I like abstracts, patterns, textures; I like to limit my compositions to a few elements, to keep them simple, uncluttered," he says, summing up his preferences.

For the past decade, Williams has divided his time between working as a park naturalist and travelling the world, and photography has played main accompaniment to both. In the case of the former, he takes photos to illustrate his slide talks and to underscore the importance of preserving our natural heritage. The camera is the only permissible means of taking something from the national parks back home with you, he stresses. As for the travel, he has brought back extensive coverage of many distant countries, Mexico, India, Nepal, Burma, and Indonesia to name a few.

"If you are a photographer, you view the world differently than most other people do," speculates Tom Yates. "You do so when you are driving to work, going on vacation, or wherever you are. You enjoy things for what they are, but you can also see them in an additional dimension."

Yates experienced the change in perceptions that the camera inspires when he returned to the Maritimes. He had lived there for several years, but had never made any photographs there. With the inquisitive eye of the photographer, he discovered a great deal that he had previously missed or overlooked.

His photo on page 109 is a specific example. "I lived in Moncton and visited that location many times, but I never noticed the seawall," he says. "It was there all along. Only when I was looking photographically, looking for designs, shapes, images, did I see it."

The picture interests him for another reason. It is made with a wide-angle lens, which he considers a favourite because it permits him to create spatial relationships not usually noticed by the eye. Most photographers would choose telephoto lenses for such a goal, since these isolate objects and seemingly compress perspective, while wide-angle lenses are thought of as best suited to do the opposite. With his 21mm lens, however, Yates abstracted the seawall by getting close to it and giving it a marked, tapering perspective.

"A photograph doesn't belong just to its maker, it belongs to the maker and the viewer; they both have something to provide in that relationship," believes Yates. Accordingly, he regularly participates in mutual criticism of work with other photographers, a process which he feels has helped him refine his skills.

"I am not so much interested in 'photography' as I am in *seeing*, in the revelations that come from truly-felt imagery," says Catherine Young.

"An excellent photograph is like any other excellent image — it awakens, reveals, disturbs, or delights — but with the additional 'kick' that you know that what is shown existed in reality. Consequently it helps us open our eyes to new ways of looking."

Young's particular way of looking at the world includes seeing it — rock, water, weather included — as a living being. It is a point of view influenced a great deal by her having spent nearly a thousand hours flying in light aircraft.

"I can hardly remember how I perceived the world before that," she reflects, "but I know I now think very geographically about *everything*. Trying to place oneself in a global context is really illuminating. It is easier to view the land as a changing, breathing body when you can fly above it and see the development from one geographical type to another. But even on the ground, it is enlightening to try to picture the difference in how, say, a wilderness area would look if it had the population density of Tokyo, or how Toronto might have looked just after the glaciers left."

Appropriately enough, Young's photo on page 75 is an aerial, but she involves herself with equal intensity in photographing small details at ground level, finding endless fascination in "the amazing diversity in the natural world on all scales."

Canada / A Landscape Portrait

Associate Editor / Sarah Reid
Designer / David Shaw
Composition / Attic Typesetting Inc.
Film Preparation and Printing by
Herzig Somerville Limited
Binding / T.H. Best Printing Co. Limited